YO-DAB-079

Daily Bread for Girls and Boys
Number 22

My body,
God's house

by Beatrice Keur
art by Sam Butcher

What is a Quiet Time?

A Quiet Time is a special time to talk with God (pray) and to let Him talk with you. Here's how this little booklet can help you in having a Quiet Time. There is a new page for every day of the month.

During your Quiet Time

1. Look for the Hide and Seek Words as you read the verses in your Bible. When you find the Hide and Seek Words, place a check mark in the square in your booklet.

2. Read the page in your booklet.

3. Talk with the Lord Jesus about what you have learned. Ask Him to help you tell someone else about Him.

I plan to have a Quiet Time with God each day.

_____

my name

_____

my special time

Hide and Seek Words ☐

As you read your Bible try to find these hidden words:

"For I [God] have created him for my glory"

Why Are We Here?

God who made the heavens and the earth also planned and made the bodies we live in. When He created the first man and woman, He said, "Let us make man in our image." He planned and made our bodies so we can see, hear, walk, work, talk and think. God knew all about us even before we were born.

Why did God make us? The answer is found in our Hide and Seek words—for His (God's) glory. He wants us to use the bodies which He made for us to please Him and bring honor to Him. That means you should use your hands, feet, eyes, lips, mind—all of yourself to please God.

Are you doing this?

As you have your Quiet Time with God each day, He will show you how to bring honor or glory to Him.

Hide and Seek Words ☐
As you read your Bible try to find these hidden words:

"I will praise thee"

How God Made Us

One day when Susan came home from school her dad met her at the door. He said, "I have a surprise for you, Susan. You have a brand new baby brother!"

Susan was so excited. She could hardly wait for the day when mother would come home from the hospital with the baby.

When she first saw her brother, he was not very big. He had very tiny feet, hands, mouth, ears and eyes. But he didn't stay tiny—he began to grow and grow. His eyes began to notice everything. One day his lips said some words. His hands took hold of Susan's fingers. His feet began to walk. With his heart he loved his big sister. As Susan watched him grow she could see how wonderfully God makes us.

Only God could make a body like yours. That is why the Hide and Seek words say, "I will praise thee."

Have you thanked God for your body?

Hide and Seek Words ☐
As you read your Bible try to find these hidden words:

"And the child grew . . ."

The Lord Jesus' Body

When the Lord Jesus, God's Son, was here upon the earth, He had a body too. The Bible tells us He was born in Bethlehem and He grew up as a boy in Nazareth.

Was His body like ours? Let's see what the Bible says. Look up these verses:

John 4:6   Jesus was t_____ .

Mark 4:38   Jesus was a_____ .

Luke 5:13   Jesus put forth His
                h_____ .

John 19:28   Jesus was t_____ .

Yes, the Lord Jesus had a body like ours, but there was one difference. He was the perfect Son of God and He had no sin. Our minds want to think bad things; our lips want to speak naughty words and our hearts and wills want to have their own way.

The Lord Jesus loves us and came to earth to save us from sin. Is He your Savior?

Hide and Seek Words ☐
As you read your Bible try to find these hidden words:

"...bare our sins in his own body on the tree"

The Lord Jesus' Body Was Hurt for Us

"God so loved the world that he gave his only begotten Son." Jesus' body suffered and died on the cross for our sins. He did this because He wants us to be with Him in Heaven someday.

The Bible says, the payment or wages of sin is *eternal death*—to be apart from God forever. The Lord Jesus loved us so much He willingly came to take our punishment for sin, so that we could have *eternal life*—to be with God forever.

A jailer once asked the missionary Paul, "What must I do to be saved?" Paul answered, "Believe on the Lord Jesus Christ and thou shalt be saved." Do you know that you have a sinful heart? Tell God about it. Believe in your heart that the Lord Jesus died for you and ask Him to come in and forgive your sin.

Did you?

Hide and Seek Words ☐

As you read your Bible try to find these hidden words:

"...ye are not your own"

Not Your Own

To whom do you belong? Your parents? Your teacher? Your country? Maybe you are thinking, *I belong to myself.* What does the Bible say? "You are not your own." That means you belong to someone else. Who is that someone else? The Lord Jesus Christ.

Jesus bought you with a price when He died on the cross for your sins and rose from the grave. Because He did all this for you the Bible says, "Glorify God in your body." How can you glorify God with your body? You can dress your

body, use your body, feed your body and take care of your body in ways that honor and please Him.

The day you received the Lord Jesus as your Savior you became His child. You are not your own. You are His. Isn't that wonderful?

Hide and Seek Words ☐

As you read your Bible try to find these hidden words:

" . . . the Spirit of God dwelleth in you"

A Dwelling Place

Fill in the blanks below with the following words:

(1) loves (2) only (3) sins (4) gave (5) life (6) we (7) eternal (8) came (9) help (10) Lord

God (1) _ _ _ _ _ us and sent His (2) _ _ _ _ Son to die on the cross for our (3) _ _ _ _ .

Jesus Christ (1) _ _ _ _ _ us and (4) _ _ _ _ His (5) _ _ _ _ for our sins that (6) _ _ might have (7) _ _ _ _ _ _ _ life.

The Holy Spirit (1) _ _ _ _ _ us and (8) _ _ _ _ to live in us to (9) _ _ _ _ us live for the (10) _ _ _ _ Jesus Christ.

Before the Lord Jesus went back to Heaven, 40 days after He rose from the grave, He made a promise. He promised to send the Holy Spirit to live in each believer. He comforts, guides, teaches and helps us to please and honor the Lord Jesus Christ. Will you let Him do these things for you?

Hide and Seek Words ☐

As you read your Bible try to find these hidden words:

"...present your bodies a living sacrifice"

A Living Sacrifice

Tom was reading his Bible and came to our verse today. "Mother, what does the word *beseech* mean?" he questioned.

Mother explained, "The word *beseech* means *to earnestly plead or beg.* Tom, the missionary Paul was writing to Christians in Rome when he said these words. He was begging them to give their bodies to God to serve Him because God was so good to them."

Mother continued. "God also wants very much for *us* to give our bodies to Him as a living sacrifice. To be a living sacrifice means we will be willing to be what God wants us to be, to do what He wants us to do and to go where He wants us to go. This is the way we show our love to Him for all He has done for us.

"Have you told God you want your life to be a living sacrifice, Tom?"

"No, but I want to right now, Mother."

WHAT ABOUT YOU?

Hide and Seek Words ☐
As you read your Bible try to find these hidden words:

" . . . it was pleasant to the eyes"

Be Careful Little Eyes

Josh was hungry. He had nothing to eat since breakfast and it was almost supper time. Hurrying home he passed an open market. Oh! Those peaches looked so good. No one was around, so he took one. What happened? Josh was *not* careful how he used his eyes.

Eve, in the garden of Eden, looked at the forbidden tree and saw that it was good for food. She saw that it was beautiful to look at. Eve took of the fruit and ate it. She was not careful how she used her eyes and so she sinned by disobeying God.

Sin often comes into our lives because of what we look at. The Bible calls it "the lust, or desires, of the eyes."

Oh, be careful little eyes what you see
There's a Savior up above
And He's looking down in love,
Oh, be careful little eyes what you see.

Are you being careful?

Hide and Seek Words ☐
As you read your Bible try to find these hidden words:

"...the seeing eye,
the Lord hath made"

Use Your Eyes to Please God

God made our eyes. They are wonderfully made and sight is very precious. We should use our eyes to please God.

Here is a quiz. Which of these things will please the Lord, when you do them? Cross out the wrong ones.

Use Your Eyes...

1. To read the Bible
2. To study your school lessons
3. To watch television when you should not
4. To see beautiful things in nature
5. To look at someone's paper during test time
6. To read dirty comic books
7. To read to Grandma or someone sick
8. To look at bad movies
9. To watch someone hurt another person
10. To look for cars before crossing the street

Prayer—Thank You God for my eyes. Help me to use them to please You. Amen.

Hide and Seek Words ☐

As you read your Bible try to find these hidden words:

"...speak for thy servant heareth"

Be Careful Little Ears

"Mike," Father shouted, "where are your ears"? Quickly Mike felt on both sides of his head. "Why! They're still here! Why did you ask me that?" This may seem funny but Father had been talking to Mike and he was not hearing. He had good ears but he was not listening. Our ears are sometime like radios. We can turn them off and on!

The boy Samuel in the Bible had his ears turned on! When God called him one night, he answered, "Speak, for thy servant heareth." Samuel listened and God told him many things and blessed him (gave him good things).

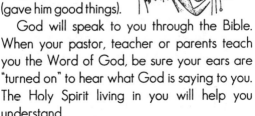

God will speak to you through the Bible. When your pastor, teacher or parents teach you the Word of God, be sure your ears are "turned on" to hear what God is saying to you. The Holy Spirit living in you will help you understand.

Hide and Seek Words ☐

As you read your Bible try to find these hidden words:

"Hear, ye children; the instruction of a father"

Listen for God

What you see and hear is what you think about. What you think about is often what you do! So it is very important that you hear and see good things.

Are you filling your mind with things that do not please God? Are you listening to dirty stories, lies and loud music that make you think wrong thoughts and do wrong things? God's

enemy, Satan, is also your enemy. He knows you belong to the Lord Jesus Christ and he will do all he can to keep you from listening to and obeying God.

God has given us His Word, the Bible, to instruct us in doing right. He has given us the Holy Spirit to teach us and help us do what the Bible says. Has God given you a father who loves God to show you how you should live?

Are you listening for God and obeying Him?

Hide and Seek Words ☐
As you read your Bible try to find these hidden words:

" . . . the tongue is a little member"

Be Careful Little Tongue

The Bible warns you to be careful how you use your tongue in speaking. The tongue is a very little member of your body, but if it is not controlled by God it can be used to say things that may do great harm. The Bible says the tongue is like a fire! It only takes one little match to start a fire that can spread and destroy many things. So, one little word can start a fight and before it is over someone may have gotten hurt very badly. The Bible says a soft answer (kind words) turn away anger.

David, who wrote the beautiful Psalms in the

Bible said, "Let the words of my mouth...be acceptable [pleasing] in thy sight, O Lord" (Psalm 19:14).

This would be a good prayer to pray each morning, don't you think?

Hide and Seek Words ☐

As you read your Bible try to find these hidden words:

"My lips shall praise thee"

Use Your Lips for God

The little maid who worked in Naaman's home used her lips to say words that pleased the Lord. Though she was a captive in a strange land and perhaps very lonely for her father and

mother, she was not afraid to tell Naaman's wife about her God. She was sure that God was able to heal Naaman of his sickness. This brought honor to God for Naaman was healed and he began to serve the true God.

It takes courage to speak for the Lord Jesus Christ. He wants you to be a witness—to tell others about Him. Perhaps some of your friends do not know that the Lord Jesus died for their sins. He would be pleased for you to be the one to tell them.

Praise the Lord with your lips—speak kindly, cheerfully, respectfully and honestly.

Hide and Seek Words ☐
As you read your Bible try to find these hidden words:

"He who hath clean hands . . . shall receive . . . blessing"

Be Careful Little Hands

I washed my hands this morning,
So very clean and white
And gave them both to Jesus
To work for Him till night.

I told my ears to listen
Quite closely all day through,
For any act of kindness
such little hands can do.

My eyes are set to watch them
About their work or play
To keep them out of mischief
For Jesus' sake all day.

The Lord Jesus wants us to have clean hands, not only clean because they have been washed with soap and water, but because they are clean from sin and do the things that please Him.

Here is a good rule to follow for using your hands—

"Whatsoever you do, do it heartily [the best you can] as to the Lord . . ." (Colossians 3:23).

Hide and Seek Words ☐

As you read your Bible try to find these hidden words:

"What is that in thine hand?"

Use Your Hands for Jesus

The Lord Jesus has a work for each one of us to do today. We all have something in our hands we can use for Him.

Moses used his shepherd's rod.

David used his slingshot.

Gideon used his clay pitcher.

Dorcas used her needle.

What about you? What do you have in your hand?

A rake to clean the yard?

A bicycle with which to do errands?

A helping hand to help some older person across the street?

A pen to write a letter?

A dollar to put in the missionary offering?

A cloth with which to do the dusting?

What do you have in your hand that you can use for the Lord Jesus? Write it on this line.

_____.

Hide and Seek Words ☐
As you read your Bible try to find these hidden words:

"...beautiful are the feet of them that preach the gospel"

Be Careful Little Feet

Sarah was hurrying just as fast as she could. She could not walk very fast. She was almost there when her pastor came walking beside her. "Sarah," he said, "you have beautiful feet." Sarah stopped. She looked at her feet and then at the pastor with questioning eyes.

"My feet are ugly," Sarah replied, "they are not beautiful." You see, Sarah was crippled. Both her feet were crooked. "How can you say they are beautiful?" she asked.

Pastor Parker looked down at her and said kindly, "God says they are beautiful because you use them for Him. You visit the sick, you do errands for older people, you come faithfully to meetings at church. Though your feet are crippled, God sees them as beautiful."

You may have good feet and can walk and run well, but can God say your feet are beautiful?

<u>Hide and Seek Words</u> ☐
As you read your Bible try to find these hidden words:

"Thy word is a lamp unto my feet"

Little Feet Be Careful

Our feet often get us into mischief, don't they? They kick your sister under the table and make her cry. They trip someone on the way to school. They go to a ball game instead of coming right home. They sneak to be with the gang rather than go to a church club. Yes, we use our feet to get us into a lot of trouble.

Have you ever walked in the dark using a

flashlight to see where you were going? Step by step you could see as the flashlight shone ahead.

God's Word is like a light or lamp to your feet to show you the right way to live. As you read and hide God's Word in your heart the Holy Spirit will show you good places to go and the right things to do. This is the way to keep your feet out of mischief.

Hide and Seek Words ☐

As you read your Bible try to find these hidden words:

"The Lord knoweth [our] thoughts"

Be Careful What You Think

It was Sarah's eighth birthday. She was so excited! "Would Mother remember? Would she make a cake?" Sarah's mind was working fast that morning.

At breakfast Mother said nothing about Sarah's birthday but hurried her off to school. Sarah was disappointed. She began to think *Mother doesn't love me. Mother is too busy to think about me.*

All day Sarah thought these wrong thoughts until she became very unhappy. She pouted all the way home. To her surprise, Mother was waiting for her. In the dining room were seven of her friends and a beautiful cake on the table! How ashamed Sarah was of her thoughts.

Did God know what Sarah was thinking all day? Yes. He knows all things, even the deepest secrets of our hearts.

Ask the Lord Jesus to put the right thoughts in your mind today.

Hide and Seek Words ☐

As you read your Bible try to find these hidden words:

"... think on these things"

Follow God's Rules

God in His Word, the Bible, has given us rules to keep our thoughts pleasing to Him. Let's see what they are!

Whatever things are

true
honest
just (right)
pure
lovely
of good report
praise to God

Think on These Things

God's Word is true, honest, just, pure, lovely, gives a good report and praises God. Does this give you a clue about what to think of each day? Yes, learning and hiding God's Word in your heart and mind is a good way to have right thoughts.

Prayer: Lord Jesus, help me to follow Your rules for good thoughts. Amen.

Hide and Seek Words ☐

As you read your Bible try to find these hidden words:

"Trust in the Lord with all thine [your] heart"

Trusting is Believing

Trust is another word for *believe*. When you sit on a chair you believe or trust the chair is strong enough to hold you. When you switch on the light you believe or trust that the light will go on.

To trust the Lord with *all* your heart means to believe and trust that He will do *all* He has said and promised in His Word, the Bible.

If you have trusted Him to be your Savior, you also need to trust Him to keep you from sinning each day. Trust Him to take care of you and help you in all you have to do.

Faith is another word for trust and believe.

> Faith is just believing (trusting)
> What God says He will do;
> He will never fail us,
> His promises are true,
> If we but receive Him
> His children we become;
> Faith is just believing (trusting)
> This wondrous thing is done.

Hide and Seek Words ☐
As you read your Bible try to find these hidden words:

" ... love the Lord ... with all thy heart"

Love Him!

We love those we trust.

To love the Lord Jesus with all your heart means to love and trust Him above everybody and everything. He must be first in your life.

The Lord Jesus loves us. He left His wonderful home in Heaven to come to earth. He took a body like ours, though He had no sin. He lived here and died on the cross for our sins and rose again so He could be our Savior. Someday He will take us to Heaven to be with Him.

"We love him [the Lord Jesus], because he first loved us" (1 John 4:19).

Hide and Seek Words ☐
As you read your Bible try to find these hidden words:

"Precious . . . are thy thoughts unto me, O God"

We are Precious to God

If you could change something about yourself, what would it be? The color of your eyes or hair? To be taller or shorter? What would it be?

Did you know that you are special to God just as you are? He made you and me and each of us special. Not one of us has even a thumb print alike. You are one of a kind.

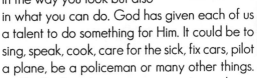

You are not only special in the way you look but also in what you can do. God has given each of us a talent to do something for Him. It could be to sing, speak, cook, care for the sick, fix cars, pilot a plane, be a policeman or many other things.

God's thoughts are precious toward you because He made you. Do not wish to be changed. Thank the Lord He made you as you are. Then, use the special talent He has given you to serve Him!

Hide and Seek Words ☐

As you read your Bible try to find these hidden words:

" . . . a certain nobleman whose son was sick"

Your Body Can Hurt

I am sure you have said, "Why do I have to be sick?"

In our Hide and Seek words today, we learn that a certain nobleman's son was sick. Sickness comes to everyone, children, grownups, rich or poor. We do not have perfect bodies. They often hurt. Why! Because of sin.

Adam and Eve, the first man and woman, had perfect bodies when God made them. They had no headaches, measles, earaches or anything else. Everything was wonderful. But when sin came into the world by their disobedience, God said their bodies would be weak and one day even die. Ever since that time there has been sickness and death.

If you have received Jesus as your Savior, someday in Heaven you will have a perfect body. Until then God wants you to take care of your body, because it is the house in which His Holy Spirit lives.

Hide and Seek Words ☐
As you read your Bible try to find these hidden words:

" . . . he would not defile himself . . . with the king's meat"

Not Only Candy

Jennifer loved candy. She begged Mother many times a day for a piece. Sometimes she even took a piece without asking. At mealtime Jennifer wasn't hungry and didn't drink her milk nor eat her food as she should. She became sick and was in the hospital a long time.

Our bodies belong to God. He wants us to take good care of them. One way to do this is to eat the right kind of foods—not only candy. When Mother says, "drink your milk and eat your vegetables," you should obey.

In the Bible, we read that Daniel decided in his heart not to eat the rich food from the king's table. It was not good for his body and it was offered to idols. Instead he asked for plain food like vegetables and water to drink. God blessed him because he chose to do this.

Hide and Seek Words ☐

As you read your Bible try to find these hidden words:

" . . . come . . . rest a while"

Oh, No! Not Yet!

The Lord Jesus had gathered His disciples (helpers) together. They had much to tell Him for they had just come back from preaching in other cities. They told Him all they had done and what they had taught. They were tired and needed to rest. The Lord Jesus knew this, so He said, "Come aside into a desert [quiet] place and rest a while."

Your body, too, needs rest. At the end of the day you are tired. Isn't it wonderful God has given you the quietness of the night to sleep and to gain new strength for the next day? Have you

ever thanked God for rest and sleep?

What do you answer when Mother or Father says, "It is bedtime." Do you say, "Okay," or "Oh, no, not yet"?

Hide and Seek Words ☐
As you read your Bible try to find these hidden words:

"Bodily exercise profiteth a little"

Exercise

We all want to grow, don't we? None of us want to stay small and weak. There are three rules we need to keep in order to grow. What are they?

1. Eat the right food
2. Get enough rest
3. Exercise

Exercise is good for you. It makes your body strong. Boys especially like to have strong muscles. They exercise each day to build them up.

You should not only want your body to grow but your spiritual life as well. How do you grow as a Christian?

Read the Bible—that is your food

Pray each day—that is your rest

Tell others about the Lord Jesus—that is your exercise

Prayer—Dear Heavenly Father, help me to take care of my body and help me to grow in my Christian life, too. In Jesus' name, Amen.

Hide and Seek Words ☐
As you read your Bible try to find these hidden words:

" . . . beholding his . . . face in a mirror"

What Does the Mirror Say?

Has Mother ever said to you, "Go look in the mirror"? Why? Did she want the mirror to tell you something?

We know mirrors do not talk, but they can tell you your face is dirty or your hair needs combing.

If your body belongs to the Lord Jesus and the Holy Spirit lives in it, shouldn't you keep your body clean?

God not only wants you to be clean on the outside but also in the inside. God's Word is like a mirror for your heart and mind. It shows you

the hate, lies, and wrong thoughts in your heart just like a mirror shows your face is dirty.

To keep clean on the outside and inside, obey the mirror on the wall *and* the mirror of God's Word!

Hide and Seek Words ☐
As you read your Bible try to find these hidden words:

"...do all to the glory of God"

What Will I Wear?

Katie was having a real hard time deciding what dress to wear to Lisa's party. The red one? The white one? If only Mother was here to help. Then she thought, *I will ask the Lord Jesus to help me decide.* She bowed her head and prayed.

Is the Lord Jesus interested in what you wear? Yes. Have you ever prayed about what you should wear? The Hide and Seek words tell

you to do all to the glory (honor) of God—even the way you dress.

I'm sure you want to honor the Lord Jesus and let others know you belong to Him. How can you do this? You can do this not only by what you say and do but how you dress. The Holy Spirit who lives in you will help you.

Hide and Seek Words ☐
As you read your Bible try to find these hidden words:

" . . . **we shall all be changed**"

In the Twinkling of an Eye

How long does it take to wink your eye? Not very long, does it?

Something wonderful is going to happen. The Lord Jesus is coming again. He will come in the "twinkling of an eye." When? We do not know. It may be today! Jesus is coming in the air to take all those who be-long to Him to Heaven.

When Christ comes, in the twinkling of an eye, your earthly body will be changed to a body that can live in Heaven. That body will never die!

Are you ready for Jesus' coming? Is He your Savior? If not, receive Him today and be ready.

Hide and Seek Words ☐
As you read your Bible try to find these hidden words:
" . . . **we shall be like him**"

A New Body

Becky is a little girl who was born blind. She has never seen her mother's or father's face. She has never seen a flower, a tree or a lake. Is she unhappy? No! Why? Because she has the Lord Jesus as her Savior. God has given her a lovely voice. She sings for Him and makes many people happy.

In Heaven everyone will have a perfect body. There will be no sickness, pain or death in Heaven. No one will be blind, crippled or deaf. Each person will have a body like the Lord Jesus.

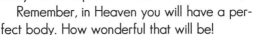

In this little book you have read about the body you now live in. You learned that God made you, Jesus bought you and the Holy Spirit lives in you. Take care of your body. Use it to please God.

Remember, in Heaven you will have a perfect body. How wonderful that will be!